Who You Callin' a Cheetah?

Printed in the United States of America

Publishing Redondo Beach, CA 90277

Despite the doctor's warnings,
George continued to use the
shampoo with extra body.

The new company president
didn't sit well with Joe.

Beethoven's Fifth Overture

"You've got only one thing on your
mind. It's always ewe, ewe, ewe."

**Sam was being groomed
for an executive position.**

**Bernie, a novice pilot,
misunderstood the control tower's
instructions to begin taxiing.**

Undentured Servant

Child Proof

Monica was jealous because Marvin
was always siding with the neighbors.

Raising Hell

**Judge Applebaum of the
Appeals Court issues a stay.**

Plain Crash

Cat Litter

Assuming a Mortgage

When Kyle entered the country,
he went through customs.

Entertaining a Motion

Snake Charmer

Bee Hooves

The clowns knew they were funny;
they just needed the right vehicle.

Victor gets the spoils.

"Every time I see Henry,
it makes my skin crawl."

Joyce called in the SWAT team.

**Three days after Gloria's operation,
doctors reintroduced solid food.**

Looking into the future, the Louisiana Hornets traded for the young second baseman and a player to be named later.

Black Tie Affair

The Reign in Spain

Window Pain

Buddha Pest

Clothes make the man.

**Historians now believe that
they never laughed at Galileo.**

To attract the great white
shark, Phillip was told to
throw his chum into the water.

Jury finds for the defendant.

Historical Moment #320
Benedict Arnold is brought
into the British camp.

Mark's grandfather raced greyhounds.

Gratuitous Violence

After 15 years of not being able to walk, Arnold's legs finally came around.

"Officer, you don't understand. He promised us swamp land in Florida."

Sensitive Nature

As usual, the tamales
disagreed with Milton.

Jerome, the orthodontist,
misunderstood the detective's
request for a large retainer.

James starts his e-business.

It was at that time
that Dr. Frankenstein
realized his mistake.

Even at an early age, teachers recognized that Sharon had a gift.

Getting An Audience With the Pope

It was only after Jay tried to
entertain the fans that he
realized he couldn't pull it off.

Irene, a gambling woman, took
the beef from the top shelf
where the steaks were higher.

People doubted Henry's
entrepreneurial skills.

Paul went to the angry plastic
surgeon who thumbed his nose.

Don refused to stand on ceremony.

Historical Moment #415
Benjamin Franklin discovers electricity.

Crack Research Team

"I think he looks quite fetching."

**Charlie takes advantage of a
customer who was born yesterday.**

Although the couples had known one another for many years, Simon and Lily had a history of their own.

That's why they paid
Bill the big bucks.

John, the personnel director
at the local bakery, worried
about the turnover rate.

Stan thought that his
promotion to captain would
give him greater visibility.

ORION THE HUNTER

LEO THE LION

TAURUS THE BULL

THE BATTLE OF HASTINGS

Jean Remberet is credited with
starting the French Resistance.

As a result of the printer's error,
Webster's life had no meaning.

Historical moment #323
Van Gogh's first telephone call.

Iron Will

Three hours after the race had
ended, Ben's whoas continued.

A Relative Unknown

Panned by the critics, Pierre
still tries to draw a crowd.

The company garnished Sid's wages.

Carbon 14

To build the new outdoor sports facility, Stratford High School hired a man with a bad track record.

Caleb hailed from the west.

Contrary to popular belief . . .

It was then that Alfred
realized that the party needed
to change its platform.

**The young Magellan
realizes his destiny.**

Raymond's relationship with his
first recliner went way back.

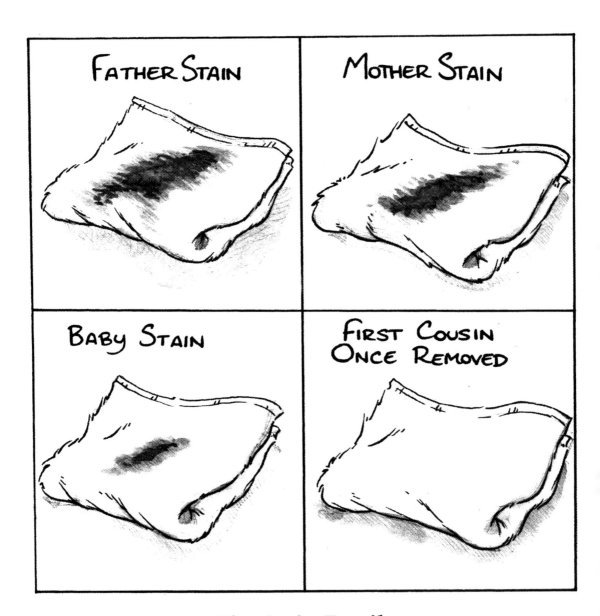

The Stain Family

For years, Martha saw
Harold behind Paula's back.

Jane could turn heads.

Historical Moment #647
The independent Columbus
asks Queen Isabella for more latitude.

Wrongful Death Suit

**Jason went to LA for
his first steady job.**